STORIES
WELL TOLD

PUBLISHED *by* Creative Education
P.O. Box 227, Mankato, Minnesota 56002
Creative Education is an imprint of The Creative Company
www.thecreativecompany.us

DESIGN AND PRODUCTION *by* Ellen Huber
ART DIRECTION *by* Rita Marshall
PRINTED *in the* United States of America

PHOTOGRAPHS *by*
Alamy (Falkenstein/Bildagentur-online Historical Collect.,
Moviestore collection Ltd, Pictorial Press Ltd, United Archives GmbH),
Corbis (Bettmann, Ted Streshinsky), Dreamstime (Oriontrail),
Getty Images (Archive Photos, Bentley Archive/Popperfoto,
Buyenlarge, Peter Dazeley, DuMont, Daniel Farson/Picture Post,
Marc Hauser Photography Ltd, Michael Ochs Archives, NBCU Photo Bank),
iStockphoto (malerapaso), Newscom (Jeff Cook/ZUMA Press),
Shutterstock (Featureflash, Johnna Evang Nonboe, RTimages),
Veer (Alloy Illustration)

Library of Congress Cataloging-in-Publication Data
Mystery / Valerie Bodden.
p. cm. — (Stories well told)
Includes bibliographical references and index.
*Summary: A survey of the mystery fiction genre, from its detective-story origins and puzzle-solving influences to
the famous authors—such as Agatha Christie—whose works have defined the genre over time.*

ISBN 978-1-60818-178-0
1. Detective and mystery stories—History and criticism—Juvenile literature. I. Title.

PN3448.D4B57 2012
809.3'872—dc23   2012023240

First Edition
2 4 6 8 9 7 5 3 1

VALERIE BODDEN

MYSTERY

CREATIVE ● EDUCATION

TABLE OF CONTENTS

A SMUDGE OF INK. A PIECE OF HAIR. THE SMELL OF COLOGNE.

— ◆ —

Sir Arthur Conan Doyle sits in his old leather armchair, mulling over the pieces of evidence he has slowly and carefully laid out. In his mind, he rearranges them, first one way and then another. Suddenly, he springs out of his chair and over to his desk, where he begins to write furiously. On the page before him, he has his character spring from his chair as well. After all, the protagonist *of his story, the great detective Sherlock Holmes, is never content to sit still for long. Doyle has written him a mystery, and Holmes must solve it, using his superb skills of* deduction *and his boundless energy for searching out clues. Holmes isn't the only one who will try to solve the puzzle, though—soon, thousands of readers will try to beat him to the solution!*

Although works that fall into the mystery genre vary widely in terms of character, action, and setting, nearly every piece of mystery fiction shares at least one element: the puzzle. And that puzzle usually takes the shape of a crime (often a murder) that needs to be solved. The protagonist of most mysteries is an investigator of some sort—professional or amateur, intelligent or tough, male or female—who attempts to solve the puzzle.

Elements of mystery can be found in works from ancient Greece and Rome, as well as in English poet Geoffrey Chaucer's landmark collection *The Canterbury Tales* (c. 1390) and French philosopher Voltaire's *Zadig: or, The Book of Fate* (1747). Even so, stories of mystery and suspense were few and far between for much of the history of Western literature. It was not until nearly the mid-19th century that the first true detective story was written. That coincided with when the first true detectives lived and worked. Among the first detectives was Frenchman François-Eugène Vidocq. A former criminal, Vidocq eventually became chief of France's first detective bureau, Le Sûreté Nationale. In 1828, Vidocq published a highly embellished account of how he went undercover, hunted down clues, and sprang traps in order to capture criminals. The book appeared in America in 1834, where it inspired the creation of a new type of tale—the detective story.

The man credited with writing the first modern detective story is American author Edgar Allan Poe, for "The Murders in the Rue Morgue" (1841). Set in Paris, this short story focuses on the horrific murder of two women. The amateur detective in the story, C. Auguste Dupin, possesses "a peculiar analytic ability," according to his admiring, unnamed associate, who narrates the story. Dupin uses that ability to deduce that the murders were committed by an orangutan that escaped from the home of a sailor who had captured it on one of his voyages. With this tale, Poe established many of the conventions that have been used in detective

< 8 >

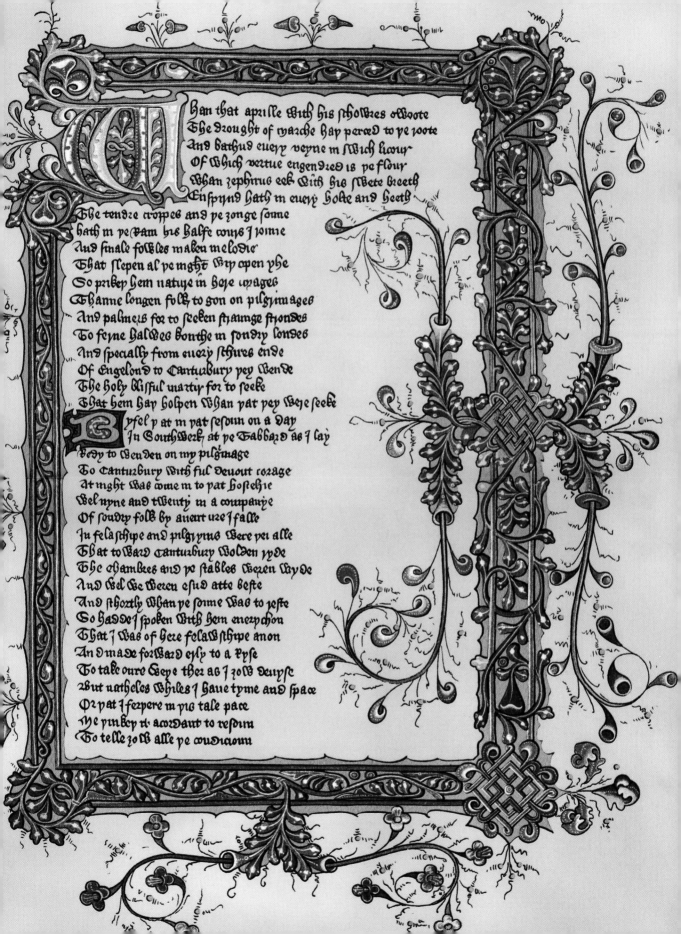

Whan that aprille with his shoures swoote
The drought of marche hath perced to ye roote
And bathud euery veyne in swich licour
Of which vertue engendred is ye flour
Whan zephirus eek with his swete breeth
Enspyrd hath in euery holte and heeth

The tendre croppes and ye zonge sonne
Hath in ye ram his halfe cours I ronne
And smale foweles maken melodie
That slepen al ye night wiy open yhe
So priketh hem nature in heye corages
Thanne longen folk to gon on pilgrimages
And palmers for to seeken straunge strondes
To ferne halwes kowthe in sondry londes
And specially from euery shires ende
Of engelond to Cantirbury yey wende
The holy blisful martir for to seeke
That hem hay holpen whan yat yey were seeke

Byfel y at in yat sesoun on a day
In Southwerk at ye Tabbard as I lay
Redy to wenden on my pilgrimage
To Cantirbury with ful deuout corage
At night was come in to yat hostelrie
Wel nyne and twenty in a companye
Of sondry folk by auent ure I falle
In felaschipe and pilgrims were yei alle
That toward Cantirbury wolden ryde
The chambres and ye stables weren wyde
And wel we weren esud atte beste
And shortly whan ye sonne was to reste
So hadde I spoken with hem euerychon
That I was of here felawschipe anon
And made forward erly to aryse
To take oure weye ther as I yow deuyse
But natheles whiles I haue tyme and space
Or yat I ferpere in yis tale pace
Me pinkey ti acordaunt to resoun
To telle yow alle ye condicioun

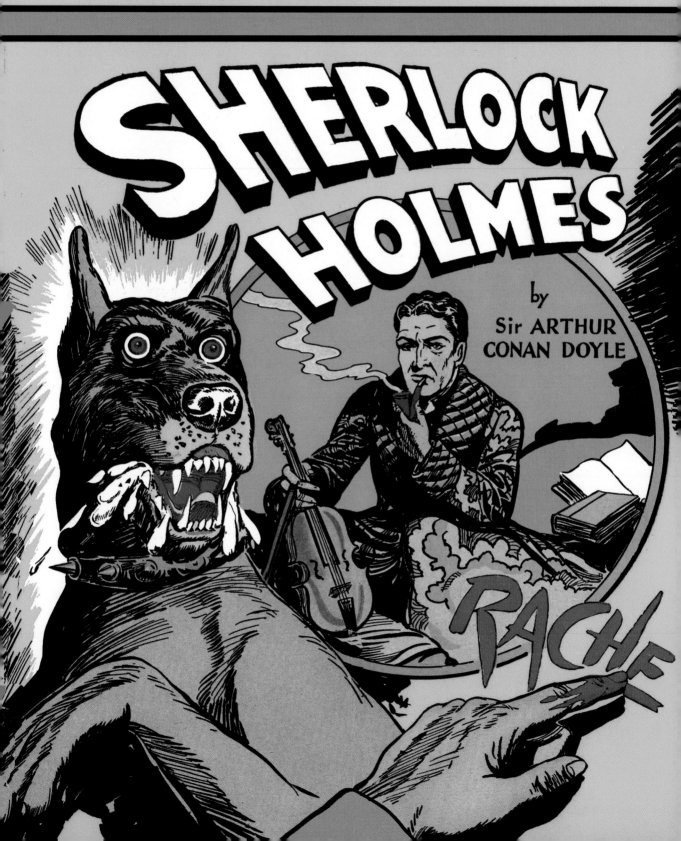

stories since that time, including, most importantly, the character of the amateur detective. "The Murders in the Rue Morgue" was followed by two other stories featuring Dupin, thus creating the first-ever mystery series—another tradition that most detective fiction would follow.

The new genre of detective fiction created by Poe was not immediately taken up by other writers, although British author Charles Dickens's novel *Bleak House* (1853) involves a detective who investigates a murder. In 1866, French writer Émile Gaboriau became the first to publish a work modeled after Poe's form, with *L'affaire Lerouge* (*The Widow Lerouge*) credited as the first true detective novel. Around the same time, new mystery stories began to appear in the United States in the form of dime novels—short, cheap paperback books that were popular with readers across the country. Simply written and action-packed, dime novels often developed into series that were hundreds of issues long.

While dime novels were usually created by anonymous writers, a new author and his detective were about to gain fame around the world. In 1887, 28-year-old Scotsman Arthur Conan Doyle published the short novel *A Study in Scarlet* in an English magazine called *Beeton's Christmas Annual*. The story introduced the character of Sherlock Holmes, who would go on to appear in 56 short stories and 3 more novels and become the most famous fictional detective of all time. Holmes's appearance on the mystery fiction scene sparked an outpouring of detective stories in both England and America.

By 1920, mystery fiction had entered a "Golden Age"—characterized by a large volume of high-quality mystery works—that would last until about 1940. Most Golden Age mysteries centered on the clue-puzzle (or the "whodunit"), a form in which the reader and the detective (almost always an amateur) compete to see who can solve the mystery first. The chief component of a clue-puzzle was the idea of

< 11 >

A MYSTERY CHARACTER

Most fictional detectives fall into one of three categories: armchair, amateur, or hard-boiled. Armchair detectives let other people do the investigating for them. They simply collect all the information and then, using their superior intellects, come up with the solution. Poe's C. Auguste Dupin is largely an armchair detective. In "The Mystery of Marie Rogêt" (1842), he relies on newspaper accounts for much of his evidence. Another famous armchair detective is American author Rex Stout's character Nero Wolfe. A large, sedentary man, Wolfe sends his assistant, Archie Goodwin, to investigate for him. Yet Archie can tell when Wolfe is pondering a case, as he describes in Over My Dead Body (1939): "[Wolfe] leaned back and ... shut his eyes.... Several times during the hour he sat there I saw his lips push in and out, so I knew he was hard at work on something."

Armchair detectives are also usually amateurs. Amateur detectives can be any age or sex, but they generally share several characteristics, including independence, a strong sense of right and wrong, good instincts, and loyalty to friends. Agatha Christie's Miss Marple and E. C. Bentley's Philip Trent are among the best-known amateur detectives. Hard-boiled detectives, by contrast, are typically loners who prefer to work on their own. They are smart but not brilliant and do not rely on their powers of deduction alone to solve a case. Most are tough—even violent—and operate by their own moral code. Raymond Chandler's Philip Marlowe is a prime example of a hard-boiled detective.

< 12 >

Hollywood actor Humphrey Bogart played the character of Philip Marlowe in the 1946 film version of Chandler's 1939 novel The Big Sleep.

fair play—an author had to provide the reader with the same clues as the detective had (although the clues could be hidden or deceptive) in order to keep the "game" fair. At the end of a clue-puzzle, the mystery was solved, with all clues and red herrings explained for the reader to follow. British author Agatha Christie's *Murder on the Orient Express* (1934), for example, concludes with the detective Hercule Poirot delivering his solution to the puzzle: "I was particularly struck by the extraordinary difficulty of proving a case against any one person on the train.... I said to myself: This is extraordinary—they cannot *all* be in it! And then, Messieurs, I saw the light. They were *all* in it.... I saw it as a perfect mosaic, each person playing his or her allotted part. It was so arranged that, if suspicion should fall on any one person, the evidence of one or more of the others would clear the accused person and confuse the issue."

Even as the Golden Age of the clue-puzzle story continued, however, a new strain of mystery fiction was beginning to develop in America, where the dime novel had been replaced by "pulp" magazines (so called because of the cheap, wood-pulp paper on which they were printed). These magazines featured a number of short stories and novelettes (short novels) in each issue. The most famous of the detective pulps was *Black Mask*, in which writers began to replace the coolly deductive amateur sleuth with tough, unsentimental private investigators (also known as "private eyes") in what came to be known as the "hard-boiled" school of crime fiction. Often, hard-boiled detectives took the law into their own hands, at times committing crimes themselves in the pursuit or capture of criminals. Hard-boiled fiction writers abandoned the leisurely pace that characterized most Golden Age works in favor of a terse, clipped, action-packed approach. That style is on display in the following excerpt from *Red Harvest* (1929) by American Dashiell Hammett, acknowledged as the founder of the hard-boiled school.

Pulp magazines paid their authors on a per-word basis and covered popular topics ranging from detectives to the military to monsters.

At five minutes after eleven, automobile brakes screeched outside. Two minutes later Mrs. Willsson came into the room. She had taken off hat and coat. Her face was white, her eyes almost black.

"I'm awfully sorry," she said, her tight-lipped mouth moving jerkily, "but you've had all this waiting for nothing. My husband won't be home tonight."...

I went away wondering why the green toe of her left slipper was dark and damp with something that could have been blood.

With its down-to-earth action, gritty detectives, and intense emotion, the hard-boiled story brought a sense of realism to the mystery genre.

By about the 1950s, the pulp magazines had begun to lose circulation and were replaced in large part by paperback books, most of which featured hard-boiled private-eye stories. In the 1970s, African American and female private eyes began to star in many series, a trend toward greater character diversity that continues today. Today's mysteries also tend to emphasize richly drawn characters over the story's puzzle—although the puzzle remains an important element. Women over the age of 45 make up the main readership of mystery novels, but the genre is so popular among men and women of all ages that it accounts for nearly 25 percent of all fiction sales in the U.S.

< 16 >

< 17 >

SORTING THROUGH THE CLUES

Although the point of a mystery story is to present a puzzle, not all mystery stories do so in the same way, and the mystery genre can be broken down into a number of subgenres (or sub-categories) because of this. Some of these subgenres are based on the type of detective featured in the story. Amateur detective stories, for example, center on unpaid sleuths who make their living outside the field of detection but often spend much of their time solving crimes. Poe's C. Auguste Dupin falls into this category. Private detective stories, on the other hand, feature protagonists who are paid for their detective work, although they do not work for an official law enforcement agency.

Detectives who work for government-sponsored agencies are featured in the police procedural, which focuses on professional police officers and the realistic, detailed steps they take to solve a crime. Rather than following a single brilliant or tough detective, the police procedural generally highlights a team of detectives as it investigates multiple crimes. In *Fiddlers* (2005) by American author Ed McBain (pseudonym of Evan Hunter), detectives Arthur Brown and Bert Kling interview a murder suspect:

> *"When's the last time you saw her alive, Mr. Shea?" Brown asked.*
>
> *"Yesterday morning. When she left for work. We had breakfast together and then … she was gone."*
>
> *"What were you doing last night around eight o'clock?" Kling asked.*
>
> *Shea said nothing for a moment. Then he said, "Is this the scene where I ask if I'm a suspect?"*
>
> *"This isn't a scene, sir," Kling said.*

Although such interrogation and information gathering may be tedious, police procedurals realistically portray it as integral to the investigation process.

Forensic scientists often use a fine black powder (or a white powder,
if the prints are on a dark surface) and a soft brush to dust for fingerprints.

Another subgenre that focuses on the law enforcement side of a mystery is the forensic novel, which features forensic scientists, such as coroners and medical examiners, who complete detailed scientific examinations of evidence. In American writer Patricia Cornwell's novel *The Last Precinct* (2000), the character Kay Scarpetta, chief medical examiner for the state of Virginia, describes her thorough examination of a victim's teeth this way: "I work a thin chisel into the side of the mouth, sliding it between molars to pry open the jaws. Steel scrapes against enamel. I am careful not to cut the lips, but it is inevitable that I chip the surfaces of the back teeth.... The dead man's jaws give up and open.... There are fibers on his tongue, and I collect them." Forensic mysteries often feature unusual murders, described in minute detail. In many cases, their protagonists, unlike real-life forensic scientists, leave the lab to track down evidence and even face villains on their own.

While some mystery subgenres are categorized according to their protagonists, others can be defined by their setting—where or when they take place. Much of the dramatic action of a courtroom mystery, for example, occurs during a court trial. In many cases, the protagonist of such works is a defense attorney attempting to prove the innocence of his or her client by identifying the true criminal. A cozy mystery is one that takes place in a limited setting (often a small town or a home) and among a small cast of characters who all know one another. Most cozy mysteries follow the pattern of the Golden Age mystery story, with an amateur detective and a focus on the puzzle. Historical mysteries take place in a realistic setting from the past— anywhere from ancient Rome to medieval Ireland or the American West.

Still other mystery subgenres are categorized based on the literary techniques employed by their authors. In an inverted mystery, for example, the author begins by showing the reader who the killer is. The puzzle in this case is not "whodunit" but rather how the detective will identify and apprehend the

A MYSTERY ACTIVITY

To readers during the Golden Age (and to many others today), the fun of reading a mystery was trying to solve the case before the detective did. Read a Golden Age mystery story (a novel by Agatha Christie or a short story by Ellery Queen, for example) to test your own skills of detection. Along the way, pay close attention to potential clues and decide who the culprit might be. Then, read the detective's conclusion. Were you right? After you have read the solution, go through the story again, making note of each clue that points to the perpetrator. Also observe any misinterpretations or red herrings that may have led you off the track. Considering all this information, do you think the author's solution was logical? Did he or she play "fair" in presenting you with all the clues you needed to solve the crime?

Now try your hand at clue-writing. Describe a scene in which a detective (amateur or professional—you decide) discovers a clue at the scene of a crime. It could be a specific object—a cigarette butt or a toothpick, for example. Or your detective might notice footprints or a unique scent. Does the clue tell your detective anything about the criminal, such as his or her gender or age or style of dress? Can your detective identify the culprit on the basis of this clue, or does he or she need more to go on? Finally, is the clue really a clue, or is it meant to lead your detective astray?

< 20 >

Different types of shoes leave prints behind on a soft surface—such as one covered by snow—and can often be identified by their tread patterns.

John Dickson Carr began his writing career in England and continued working even after suffering a stroke that paralyzed the left side of his body.

criminal. And in the locked-room mystery, the crime occurs under seemingly impossible circumstances. Poe's "The Murders in the Rue Morgue" was the first locked-room mystery, as one of its victims was found in a room that had been locked from the inside. In the 20th century, American author John Dickson Carr gained a reputation as a master of the locked-room mystery. In his 1965 novel *The House at Satan's Elbow*, the character of Pennington Barclay tells his nephew Nick of a strange figure who fired a revolver at him and then escaped through the window. Yet this appears to Nick to have been impossible:

> *"But the window's closed! Look here!"*

> *"My visitor—or visitant—could have closed it as he went. Those windows slide easily in their grooves, and the rest of you were making a good deal of noise."*

> *"Uncle Pen, look! Couldn't this joker have hidden behind the curtains, and waited a moment or so, and then slipped away through the room when you weren't looking?"*

> *"No, Nick, he could not!… What's the matter with you?"*

> *Nick took a step towards him.*

> *"I'll tell you what's the matter…. This window is locked on the inside."*

The locked room requires the detective—and reader—to figure out not only *who* committed the crime but also *how* they did so.

Mystery stories have been so popular with audiences of all ages that many authors have developed young adult, or juvenile, mysteries just for teens. These stories often feature teenage protagonists, such as the brothers Frank and Joe Hardy—known as the Hardy Boys—or the fearless sleuth Nancy Drew. In this scene from *The Clue in the Old Stagecoach* (1960) by Carolyn Keene (a pseudonym for several different authors), Nancy and her friend George (a girl) come face-to-face with the bad guys.

> *Just as the two girls walked up to the old stagecoach, a man's deep voice*
> *commanded harshly, "Stand where you are!"*
>
> *Their hearts pounding, Nancy and George stood stock-still. Though both had been*
> *startled by the command from the unseen speaker, the girls tried not to show any fear.*
>
> *"Who are you?" Nancy asked her hidden opponent. The man did not reply to her*
> *question. Instead, he ordered the girls to retrace their steps.*
>
> *"Why?" Nancy countered, trying to stall for time....*
>
> *"Do as I say!" the stranger growled.*

While the majority of mystery works in the past 80 years have been in the novel form, the genre got its start in the short story. Poe's first mysteries, of course, were short stories, as were the majority of the Sherlock Holmes tales. By the late 1930s, however, authors and publishers began to turn from the short story form, which could be just as demanding to write as a longer work, but with less space to develop the plot. Many writers came to prefer the slower pace of the novel, which allowed them to lay out clues and build suspense until the point of the final revelation—a scene that in itself might be the length of an entire short story. Even so, mystery short stories continue to be written, and many of them are today published in *Ellery Queen's Mystery Magazine*, which was founded in 1941 by American mystery writer Ellery Queen (a pseudonym for cousins Frederic Dannay and Manfred B. Lee).

< 24 >

Although widely recognized as the father of the detective story, Edgar Allan Poe wrote only three mysteries. The majority of the rest of his short stories fall into the horror genre. Yet, in his three detective stories, Poe laid out the basic pattern of the genre, with its focus on a crime and the man (or woman) who must solve it. Poe's "The Murders in the Rue Morgue" was published in *Graham's Magazine*, of which he was the editor, in April 1841. With its horrific murders (one victim stuffed up a chimney, the other nearly beheaded), eccentric detective C. Auguste Dupin (who ventures out of the house only at night), and surprise ending (the killer is an orangutan), the story captured the public's imagination. Its widespread popularity led Poe to write two more tales featuring Dupin: "The Mystery of Marie Rogêt" (1842), heavily based on an unsolved murder that actually occurred in New York, and "The Purloined Letter" (1845). Sometimes referred to as Poe's tales of ratiocination, or logical thinking, his detective stories paved the way for future mystery writers.

Poe's mysteries had a strong influence on Sir Arthur Conan Doyle, as did the observational and deductive skills of one of Doyle's medical school professors, Dr. Joseph Bell. When he began to write *A Study in Scarlet*, Doyle gave Bell's skills to his detective protagonist, Sherlock Holmes. Although the first Holmes story was not a wild success, it gave rise to one of the best-known characters of all time. Like Poe's Dupin, Holmes is a brilliant, though odd, detective. He lives at 221B Baker Street with Dr. Watson, his admiring assistant, who records not only Holmes's brilliant deductions but also his character behind the doors of his home: he is a pipe-smoking intellectual, with interests that range from the opera to forensic science. In addition to his astounding deductive skills, Holmes is a man of action, willingly facing poisonous snakes and fiendish criminals alike. Although Doyle tried to kill off his protagonist in "The Final Problem" (1893), as Holmes and his archenemy,

< 26 >

The 1932 film Murders in the Rue Morgue starred Bela Lugosi,
whose heavy Hungarian accent made him sound convincingly ominous.

The mysterious circumstances surrounding the death of Sigsbee Manderson,
played by Orson Welles in 1952's Trent's Last Case, *confuse Philip Trent.*

Professor Moriarty, tumble over a waterfall together, public outcry led Doyle to bring the character back in 1902. He went on to write Sherlock Holmes stories until 1927. Like Poe, Doyle influenced nearly every detective writer to follow, and Sherlock Holmes is among the most imitated and parodied characters in fiction.

Despite the popularity of brilliant, infallible detectives such as Holmes and Dupin, in the early 20th century, British writer E. C. Bentley decided that he could improve on the detective story. The newspaper journalist wanted to create a protagonist "who was recognizable as a human being," one who made mistakes, participated in society, and was capable of demonstrating feelings. He did this with the character of Philip Trent, an amateur detective first introduced in *Trent's Last Case* (1913). Unlike the unerring Holmes, Trent comes to the wrong conclusion and even falls in love with the lead suspect. At the end of the case, Trent is shocked to learn the killer's identity.

> *"It can't be!" [Trent] exploded....*
>
> *Mr. Cupples, busy with his last mouthful, nodded brightly.... "It's very simple," he said. "I shot Manderson myself."*
>
> *"I am afraid I startled you," Trent heard the voice of Mr. Cupples say. He forced himself out of his stupefaction like a diver striking upward for the surface.... He drew a deep breath, which was exhaled in a laugh wholly without merriment. "Go on," he said.*

This conclusion is as much a shock to the reader—who has not been provided with all the clues along the way—as it is to Trent.

Agatha Christie, by contrast, made sure that her readers could solve the mystery along with her detectives, provided that they picked up on and correctly interpreted the clues. Even so, the solutions to her clue-puzzles were often a

< 29 >

A MYSTERY MASTER

Born in Maryland in 1894, Dashiell Hammett quit school at the age of 13, working at a number of odd jobs before beginning an 8-year career as a private investigator with the Pinkerton National Detective Agency. Pinkerton agents relied on criminal informants, methodical investigations, instinct, and cunning in order to solve cases, and when he began writing mysteries, Hammett incorporated these elements into his works, producing the first hard-boiled detective stories.

Hammett's earliest hard-boiled works were pulp stories featuring a character known as the Continental Op (short for Operative). His first two novels, Red Harvest and The Dain Curse, both published in 1929, also followed the exploits of the Continental Op, who kills and injures many villains in the course of his investigations. Widely regarded as Hammett's best novel, The Maltese Falcon (1930) introduced a new, harder detective in Sam Spade, whom Hammett once described as "a dream man in the sense that he is what most of the private detectives I worked with would like to have been and in their cockier moments thought they approached. For your private detective ... wants to be a hard and shifty fellow, able to take care of himself in any situation." The character of the hardened private eye was taken up by countless writers after Hammett, making him one of the most influential writers in the mystery genre. Upon his death in 1961, The New York Times recognized his contributions to the genre, referring to the author as "the dean of the so-called 'hard-boiled' school of detective fiction."

Humphrey Bogart, as Sam Spade, popularized the character type of the hard-boiled detective in Hollywood crime dramas known as film noir.

surprise, with the least likely character proving to be the culprit. In one case (*The Murder of Roger Ackroyd*, 1926), the murderer even proves to be the story's first-person narrator. Christie wrote her first novel, *The Mysterious Affair at Styles* (1920), at the age of 26 while also working as a pharmacist. The novel features the detective Hercule Poirot, who must investigate a poisoning. (Christie's pharmaceutical job gave her knowledge of poisons, which she used in this and many other works.) Altogether, Christie wrote more than 70 novels and nearly 160 short stories, many featuring Poirot and others starring Miss Jane Marple, a character inspired by friends of the author's grandmother. Christie's prolific output, along with her mastery of the clue-puzzle form, earned her the nicknames "Queen of Crime" and "Duchess of Death."

Like Christie, English author Dorothy L. Sayers created clue-puzzles. Sayers's amateur detective, Lord Peter Wimsey, is a well-developed character: educated, cultured, and snobbish, wearing fine clothes and enjoying fast cars. Although Sayers's novels, which are set in the 1920s and '30s, include murder, they do not describe gore but rather focus on character interactions and breezy dialogue, as in this scene from *The Unpleasantness at the Bellona Club* (1928).

> *"Hullo!"*
>
> *"Is that you, Wimsey? Hullo! I say, is that Lord Peter Wimsey. Hullo! I must speak to Lord Peter Wimsey. Hullo!"*
>
> *"All right. I've said hullo. Who're you? And what's the excitement?"*
>
> *"It's me. Major Fentiman. I say—is that Wimsey?"*
>
> *"Yes. Wimsey speaking. What's up?"*
>
> *"I can't hear you."*

< 32 >

Actress Angela Lansbury starred as Miss Marple in the 1980 film
The Mirror Crack'd, *which was based on an earlier Christie novel.*

Ellery Queen stories were adapted for television in the 1950s, with

"Of course you can't if you keep on shouting. This is Wimsey. Good morning.

Stand three inches from the mouthpiece and speak in an ordinary voice. Do not say

hullo! To recall the operator, depress the receiver gently two or three times."

Wimsey's humor was one of the characteristics that made him so likeable to readers—and to his doting author, who gained a reputation not only for her mystery stories but also for her commentaries on the genre.

In America, the Golden Age mystery was taken up by a number of writers, including those who wrote under the pen name of Ellery Queen. "Ellery Queen" was also the name of a fictional amateur detective. The character was introduced in *The Roman Hat Mystery* (1929), written for a detective fiction contest (which it won). Ellery Queen stories featured elaborate plots, which, like other novels of the Golden Age, laid out clues for the reader to follow. At the end of many stories, Queen even issued a direct challenge to readers before offering the solution, as in this line from *The Roman Hat Mystery*: "The alert student of mystery tales, now being in possession of all the pertinent facts, should at this stage in the story have reached definite conclusions on the questions propounded." Queen stories adapted over the 40-year course of the series to keep up with the changing style of the detective novel. While the earliest works depict Queen as an intellectual, self-absorbed, and fearful man (scared even of guns), in later works, many of these characteristics are eliminated from Queen's personality altogether. The stories themselves also began to include psychological, social, and political elements. The American public appreciated Queen's unique characteristics; throughout the 1930s and '40s, he was the best-known detective in the country.

< 35 >

By the 1920s, many American authors began to turn from the cool logic of the Golden Age mystery as the hard-boiled school of detective fiction emerged in pulp magazines. Among the masters of hard-boiled fiction was American author Raymond Chandler, who got his start with the short story "Blackmailers Don't Shoot," published in *Black Mask* magazine in 1933, when Chandler was 45 years old. Most of Chandler's works feature the private detective Philip Marlowe, a tough guy who is also intelligent, honorable, and surprisingly sensitive. Marlowe narrates his own story in a distinctive first-person voice, giving the reader direct access to his thoughts. (The technique proved so successful that most other American detective writers would adopt the same style.) Chandler's works were noted for their vivid descriptions and rich figurative language, as in this description of a drive along the California coast from *Farewell, My Lovely* (1940): "There was loneliness and the smell of kelp and the smell of wild sage from the hills. A yellow window hung here and there, all by itself, like the last orange. Cars passed, spraying the pavement with cold white light, then growled off into the darkness again. Wisps of fog chased the stars down the sky." Chandler's literary focus helped to elevate the hard-boiled subgenre in the eyes of critics and set the standard for future writers.

Belgian-French author Georges Simenon combined features of the American hard-boiled school with a French-inspired focus on psychological realism to create one of the best-known detectives of the era, Jules Maigret. Chief inspector of the French Police Judiciaire, Maigret was introduced in *The Strange Case of Peter the Lett* (1931). Often relying on intuition to solve a crime, Maigret focuses on understanding the criminal mind and even forms a strong emotional bond with many of the criminals he investigates. As a result, he is often left with mixed feelings when he apprehends them. After Maigret extracts a confession

< 36 >

Robert Mitchum's portrayal of the fictional detective Philip Marlowe in 1975's
Farewell, My Lovely stays true to the character's honest, tough-guy persona.

from the suspect John Arnold in *Maigret and the Millionaires* (1958), for example, a young police officer watches Maigret leave the room, noting that the detective "as he went by, laid his hand for an instant, as though absentmindedly, on John Arnold's shoulder." All told, Maigret appeared in 83 novels and 28 short stories, as Simenon wrote at an astounding pace, sometimes completing an entire novel in less than a week.

Appearing around the same time as Philip Marlowe and Jules Maigret was another character who would achieve great fame: Perry Mason. Mason was the creation of American Erle Stanley Gardner, an attorney-turned-writer who became one of the best-selling authors of the mid-20th century. Gardner, who began publishing in the pulp magazines in the 1920s, introduced Mason in *The Case of the Velvet Claws* in 1933 and eventually wrote more than 80 novels featuring the character. Like Gardner, Mason is an attorney, and much of the action in a Perry Mason story takes place in the courtroom, where Mason proves the innocence of his clients by identifying the true perpetrators. Such dramatic scenes made the Perry Mason series ideal for radio, television, and film adaptations.

While Gardner rejected the label of hard-boiled fiction for his mysteries, American author Ross Macdonald (pseudonym of Kenneth Millar) introduced a new hard-boiled detective, Lew Archer, in 1949, with *The Moving Target*. Archer went on to star in 17 more novels. Reflecting Macdonald's own experience with psychotherapy, these psychologically intricate works often feature dysfunctional families, whose history Archer must investigate in order to solve multiple crimes (many committed long ago). Often, the criminal proves to be a middle-class woman who has been victimized in some way. In *Sleeping Beauty* (1973), for example, Marian Lennox kills her husband's mistress, telling Archer, "You men are dirty creatures, all of you. I'm glad all this has come out. I've been sick of this filthy

A MYSTERY CLASSIC

Often critically acclaimed as the best Sherlock Holmes novel, The Hound of the Baskervilles *was originally published as a series of stories in* Strand Magazine *in 1901 and 1902. In this novel, Holmes investigates the death of Sir Charles Baskerville, whose body was found outside his home with paw prints surrounding it. It appears that he has been a victim of the Baskerville curse—a curse that involves haunting by a supernatural black hound.*

Remaining out of sight during the early part of the investigation so as not to warn the murderer, Holmes pieces together the mystery. He sets a trap to capture the killer, who is now after Sir Henry Baskerville, Sir Charles's heir. Hiding on the nearby moor as Sir Henry walks home one evening, Holmes and Watson encounter the legendary beast: "A hound it was, an enormous coal-black hound, but not such a hound as mortal eyes have ever seen. Fire burst from its open mouth, its eyes glowed with a smouldering glare, its muzzle and hackles and dewlap were outlined in flickering flame." After killing the creature, Holmes discovers why it looks so fiendish: it has been painted with phosphorus (a chemical that glows). Holmes later reveals that the killer was Mr. Jack Stapleton, who has been found drowned on the moor. Stapleton, the Baskervilles' neighbor, was also a relative in disguise and was in line to inherit the estate. Although written more than 100 years ago, The Hound of the Baskervilles *continues to be widely read today and has been adapted into a number of films.*

< 40 >

THE HOUND
· OF THE ·
BASKERVILLES

BY A. CONAN DOYLE
PRICE 6/-

GEORGE NEWNES LTD.

The first book edition of
The Hound of
the Baskervilles
was published in England by
George Newnes in 1902.

pretense of a marriage for years." As Archer listens to her confession, he notices her detachment: "Her voice was cold and resentful. She had suffered so much that she was immune to anyone else's suffering." The Archer novels were critically acclaimed for their depth of character as well as their flowing prose.

By 1964, American author John D. MacDonald had already published 43 novels, but that year he began a new series with *The Deep Blue Good-by*, featuring the protagonist Travis McGee. A self-described "salvage consultant," McGee finds and recovers stolen goods for clients, usually innocent young women who have been swindled in one way or another. McGee seeks to defend the women's honor—serving as a modern knight of sorts. Appearing in 21 novels between 1964 and 1985, McGee became one of the most popular detectives of the time, and through him, MacDonald chronicled the changing times of contemporary American society.

Although he began his writing career penning Westerns, American author Elmore Leonard turned to detective fiction after riding along with a homicide police squad, releasing his first crime novel, *The Big Bounce*, in 1969. Unlike most mystery writers, who compose in series, Leonard creates new characters for nearly every book, rendering each in a unique voice. He also often uses multiple points of view, allowing several characters to offer their versions of the story. In many instances, this allows the reader to know more about the case than the other characters do; readers may even be allowed to observe the crime and enter into the mind of the villain. Known as the "Dickens from Detroit," Leonard is noted for his realistic portrayals of contemporary people and places and for his true-to-life dialogue.

Until the 1980s, the majority of hard-boiled detectives were men. Then, in 1982, American author Sue Grafton published *"A" is for Alibi*, inspired, she said, by her own fantasies of poisoning her ex-husband. The novel became the

< 42 >

Elmore Leonard worked for an advertising agency for 12 years while getting his start as a published author, quitting only after his books were a success.

Michael C. Hall plays bloodstain pattern analyst and serial killer Dexter Morgan on the television series **Dexter,** *based on Jeff Lindsay's novels.*

first in a series of alphabetically titled books that had reached *"V" is for Vengeance* by 2011. The series features private investigator Kinsey Millhone, who, like most of her hard-boiled male predecessors, is tough and independent, often facing direct danger from the criminals she investigates. At the same time, Millhone is a humorous character with believable flaws, such as an addiction to fast food—traits that have endeared her to millions of readers.

Both Leonard and Grafton continue to publish mysteries, and they are joined by a new generation of authors. While some writers have reworked the Golden Age mystery for modern times, others, such as American author Jeff Lindsay (pseudonym of Jeffry P. Freundlich), are pushing the hard-boiled novel to new extremes. Lindsay's protagonist, Dexter Morgan, is not a typical detective. In fact, he is a serial killer. But he controls his urges to kill innocent victims by searching out other murderers, whom he then kills.

Although the mystery genre has gone through many changes since Poe wrote "The Murders in the Rue Morgue," most mystery stories still contain many of the elements found in that first tale: a murder, an investigator, and a puzzle. From the brilliant amateur sleuth to the tough private eye, the genre has introduced some of the most memorable characters in fiction, including Sherlock Holmes and Philip Marlowe. Relying on logic, investigation, psychological profiling, and, sometimes, just plain instinct, those detectives—and their readers—have engaged in a single-minded pursuit: the solution to the mystery.

< 45 >

amateur: a person who does something as a hobby or pastime rather than as a paid job

contemporary: living or existing at the same time as someone or something else

deduction: the process of coming to a conclusion based on the evidence available

diversity: variety in gender, age, or ethnicity

figurative: not literal but implying something other than what is said

first-person: a point of view in which a character tells his or her own story, using the pronouns "I" or "we"

forensic: having to do with the use of science to investigate crimes

genre: a category in which a literary work can be classified on the basis of style, technique, or subject matter

infallible: incapable of failure or mistakes

informants: people who provide damaging information against others to the police or other investigators

moor: a wild, treeless, often marshy area of land covered with plants such as heather, coarse grasses, or moss

parodied: copied or imitated in a humorous way

points of view: the perspectives from or attitudes with which the narrators of a literary work see events

protagonist: the main character in a work of fiction

pseudonym: a made-up name, often used by an author in place of his or her real name

psychological: having to do with the mind and effects on the mind

psychotherapy: the treatment of mental disorders through psychological methods, such as counseling

red herrings: irrelevant or misleading clues intended to deflect attention or cause confusion

supernatural: relating to objects or powers that have no natural explanation and seem to exist outside natural laws

Western: coming from or having to do with the part of the world that includes Europe and North and South America, where culture has been influenced by ancient Greek and Roman civilizations as well as Christianity

< 46 >

WEBSITES

Edgar Allan Poe Museum: Students
http://www.poemuseum.org/students.php
Learn more about Edgar Allan Poe, and try to solve the mystery of his death.

Hardy Boys Online
http://www.hardyboysonline.net/content.php?page=home
Gain insight into the world of the Hardy Boys by reading about the characters, cases, and series.

MysteryNet's Kids Mysteries
http://kids.mysterynet.com/
Follow the clues to solve the latest case and read other mystery stories.

Writing with Writers: Mystery Writing
http://teacher.scholastic.com/writewit/mystery/index.htm
Author Joan Lowery Nixon acts as guide in this online mystery-writing workshop.

Every effort has been made to ensure that these sites are suitable for children, that they have educational value, and that they contain no inappropriate material. However, because of the nature of the Internet, it is impossible to guarantee that these sites will remain active indefinitely or that their contents will not be altered.

SELECTED BIBLIOGRAPHY

Bloom, Harold, ed. *Classic Mystery Writers*. New York: Chelsea House Publishers, 1995.

Collins, Max Allan. *The History of Mystery*. Portland, Ore.: Collectors Press, 2001.

Kelleghan, Fiona, ed. *100 Masters of Mystery and Detective Fiction*. Pasadena, Calif.: Salem Press, 2001.

Niebuhr, Gary Warren. *Make Mine a Mystery: A Reader's Guide to Mystery and Detective Fiction*. Westport, Conn.: Libraries Unlimited, 2003.

Rollyson, Carl, ed. *Critical Survey of Mystery and Detective Fiction*. 5 vols. Pasadena, Calif.: Salem Press, 2008.

Saricks, Joyce. *The Readers' Advisory Guide to Genre Fiction*. Chicago: American Library Association, 2001.

Waugh, Hillary. *Hillary Waugh's Guide to Mysteries & Mystery Writing*. Cincinnati, Ohio: Writer's Digest Books, 1991.

Winks, Robin W., ed. *Detective Fiction: A Collection of Critical Essays*. Englewood Cliffs, N.J.: Prentice-Hall, 1980.

< 47 >

< 48 >